Meg goes t

M000024972

Rigby
A Harcourt Achieve Imprint

www.Rigby.com
1-800-531-5015

My doll is in bed.

My teddy is in bed.

My rabbit is not in bed.

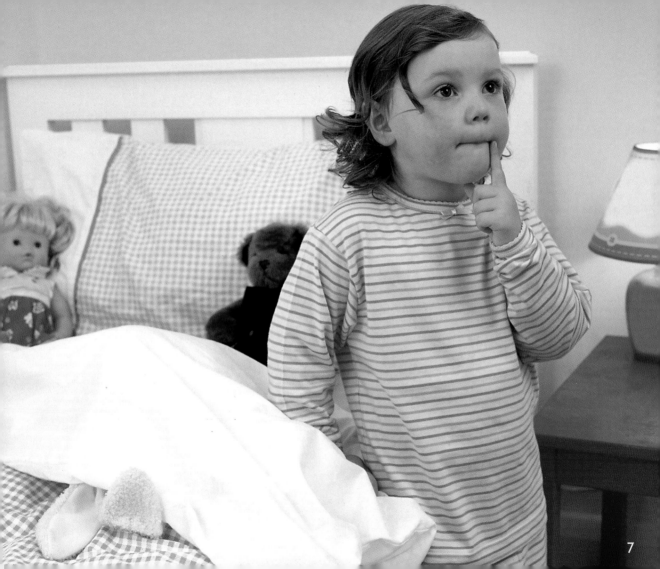

I am looking for my rabbit.

My rabbit is not in here.

My rabbit is not in here.

Here is my rabbit.

My rabbit is in bed.

I am in bed, too.